Sense POETRY

Across the Globe

Edited by Donna Samworth

First published in Great Britain in 2016 by:

Young Writers

Remus House
Coltsfoot Drive
Peterborough
PE2 9BF
Telephone: 01733 890066
Website: www.youngwriters.co.uk

All Rights Reserved
Book Design by Spencer Hart
© Copyright Contributors 2016
SB ISBN 978-1-78624-240-2

Printed and bound in the UK by BookPrintingUK
Website: www.bookprintinguk.com

Foreword

Dear Reader,

Welcome to this book packed full of sights
and smells, sounds and tastes!

Young Writers' Sense Poetry competition was specifically designed for Key Stage 1 children as a fun introduction to poetry and as a way to think about their senses: what the little poets can see, taste, smell, touch and hear in the world around them. From this starting point the poems could be as simple or as elaborate as the writer wanted, using imagination and descriptive language to conjure a complex image of the subject of their writing, rather than concentrating just on what it looks like.

Given the young age of the entrants we have tried to include as many poems as possible. Here at Young Writers we believe that seeing their work in print will inspire a love of reading and writing and give these young poets the confidence to develop their skills in the future. Poetry is a wonderful way to introduce young children to the idea of rhyme and rhythm and helps learning and development of communication, language and literacy skills.

These young poets have used their creative writing abilities, sentence structure skills, thoughtful vocabulary and, most importantly, their imaginations to make their poems come alive. I hope you enjoy reading them as much as we have.

Jenni Bannister

Editorial Manager

Looks like you're in for a treat!

Contents

Arjun Sawant (7) 1
Umamah Batool Hussain (5) 1
Vinuga Perera (5) 2
Natalia Tyl (5) 2
Fred Patterson (7) 3
Mia Page (6) 4
Kassian Rus (6) 4
Maariyah Maravia (6) 5
Dhriti Manjunath (5) 5
Nathan Peter Lee (6) 6
Elias Taher (5) 6
Kajal Patel (6) 7

Alderbury & West Grimstead CE VA School, Salisbury

Olivia Thorpe (5) 7
Emily Linton (5) 8
Jayden Moody (5), Ryan King (6), Freya, Poppy, Oscar, Max, Amber & Greg 9

Assunnah Primary School, London

Yusuf Aden (5) 9
Tasneem Jama (6) 10
Riham Mubarak (5) 10
Nusayba Nsubuga (6) 11
Mohamed Amin Mahmoud (5) 11
Mazin Abbas (6) 12
Fardowsa Abdikadir (5) 12

Avonmore Primary School, London

Subhan Qasimi (6) 13
Angelina Tarabay (6) 13
Anna Casali (7) 14
Auriana Barboza (6) 14
Daniel O'Mahony (6) 15
Dobroslav Kiselev (6) 15
Elizabete Kuduma (6) 16
Forozan Azizi (6) 16
Isla Shaw (7) 17
Jasmin Zielinska (6) 17
Lana Jaukovic (6) 18
Mattewos Zelalem (7) 18
Mosab Khalid Abdullahi (7) 19
Noor Kazim (7) 19
Pearl Ida (6) 20
Riley Phillpot-Power (6) 20
Ronny Totraku (6) 21

Bembridge CE Primary School, Bembridge

Henry McDonald (6) 21
Gabriel Ellingson (5) 22
Molly Tattersall (5) 22
Joshua Young (5) 23
Ellis Yardley (5) 23
Mia Cutting (5) 24
Amelia Dutch (6) 24
Max Williams (6) 25
Ebon Huxley Noall (6) 25
Dylan Wightwick (6) 26
Charlie Michael Duggan (5) 26
Aoife Bradley (6) 27
Jessica Taylor (6) 27
Tani Brooks (6) 28

Crown Wood Primary School, Bracknell

Isla Young (7) 28
Bryony Thompson (6) 29
Frankie Garner (6) 29
Keira Lee (7) 30
Freya Brooks (7) 30
Harley Fordham (6) 31
Jamie Newstead (7) 31
Jayden Denzil Bradbury (6) 32

Cullingworth Village Primary School, Bradford

Olivia Stafford-Bennett (6)	32
Macsen Morris (5)	33
Lyla Illingworth (5)	33
Lucy Walker (5)	34
Lily Diamond (6)	34
Finlay Gardner (5)	35
Ava-Jean McTurk (5)	35
Angelina Gloire Rumwagira (5)	36
Madison Parkinson (6)	36
Zoey Lauren Ross (6)	37
Isabelle Holdsworth (5)	37
Jack Bennett (6)	38

Gatten And Lake Primary School, Shanklin

Dylan Cooper (7)	38
Holly Paxton-Ford (6)	39
Rubi Anne Harper (6)	39
Michael Manning (5)	40
Nicole Amy Clio Beale (6)	40
Jayden Russell	41
Rosie Tayler (6)	41
Diana Madaras	42
Reggie-Joe Brown (6)	42
Vinnie Ray Dennis (6)	43
Enes Yigit Korkmaz	43
Harry English	44
Olivia Bird	44
Charlotte Emily Page (6)	45
Chloe Elizabeth Welsh (6)	45
Grace Robinson (7)	46
Julia Blok (6)	46
Matthew Moralee (6)	47
Ruby Jones (7)	47
Alfie Beeney (7)	48
Amber Sheaff (6)	48
Aiden Beckley (7)	49
Jessica Louise Moore (6)	49
Marley Samuel Dyer (6)	50
Matthew Manning (7)	50
Cailub Harbour (7)	51
Phoebe Arnold (7)	51

Harlesden Primary School, London

Qaid Al Aswad (6)	52
Genius Cowans (5)	52
Nuhad Hasan Khan (5)	53
Mijuwada Parambil (6)	53

Heriot Primary School, Paisley

Ellie Louden (8)	54
Ewan Murray (7)	54
Ewan Jamieson (7)	55
Hannah McCallum (7)	55
Eva Lousie Slimmon (7)	56
Riley Meechan (7)	56
Sophie Karen Help (8)	57
Morgan Gallacher (7)	57
Keira Abbie Quinn (7)	58
Richard McKnight (8)	58
Marcus Issac (7)	59
Jamie Hunter (7)	59
Hayden Hodgkinson (8)	60
Jamie McKechnie (7)	60

Jumeirah English Speaking School, Dubai

Zoe Whitaker	61
Azarin Jalaei (7)	61
Ayanna Sethi (7)	62
Shreya Kopuri	62
Asta Maddox (7)	63
Jodyn Foong (6)	64
Thomas Ding	65

Keiss Primary School, Wick

Isla Jack (5)	65
Zoe Mackay (6)	66
Tyler Campbell (7)	66
Alexander Mackay (6)	67
Aimee Lowe (6)	67
Ella-May Merry (6)	68
Callum Booth (5)	68
Islay Anderson (6)	69
Caitlyn Fitzimmons (5)	69
Loïc Manson (5)	70

Kingshill Infant School, Ware

Tilly Thorpe ... 70
William Glenister ... 71
Felix Flanagan ... 71
Zoe Boldick (6) ... 72
Poppy Booth ... 72
Maisie Draper (5) ... 73
Callum Glover ... 73
Isabel-Rose Haldenby (6) ... 74
Chloe Rose Abraham (5) ... 74
Lottie Hill ... 75
Erin Bellamy (5) ... 75
Coby Friedner (6) ... 76
Bow Tierney ... 76
Finn O'Neill (6) ... 77
Mabel Farrell (5) ... 77
Isabel Hall (6) ... 78
Ioan Rhys James (5) ... 78
Morten Tveit (5) ... 79
Bethany Lippiatt (6) ... 79
Harry Samuel (6) ... 80
Abbey Johnson (5) ... 80
Holly May Kimpton (6) ... 81
Neave Baker (5) ... 81
Evie Grace Crolla (6) ... 82
Erin Bartholomew (5) ... 82
Ethan Neighbour (5) ... 83
Olly Gumble (6) ... 83
Harry Watson (5) ... 84
Emily Jay Bourne (5) ... 84

Leslie Primary School, Glenrothes

Ruby Garside (7) ... 85
Josh Taylor (7) ... 85
Joss McKinlay (7) ... 86
Peyton Gillespie (7) ... 86
Emma McIntyre (7) ... 87
James Wilson (7) ... 87
Idris Mowbray (7) ... 88
Brooke Gibson (7) ... 88
Charley Rutherford Gallacher (7) ... 89
Connor Blackie (7) ... 89
Deren Mede (7) ... 90

Cole Senkel (7) ... 90
Mason Ross (6) ... 91
Murron Pratt (6) ... 91
Mikolaj Krzysztof Zubowicz (6) ... 92
Lucy Dryburgh (6) ... 92
Libby Milne (6) ... 93
Keira Simpson (6) ... 93
Josh Gorrie (6) ... 94
Freya Jane Stewart (6) ... 94
Charley Cockburn (6) ... 95
Connor Westie (6) ... 95
Brandon Baird (6) ... 96
Alix Casey (6) ... 96

Manor Fields Primary School, Salisbury

Jaime-Leigh Tyler/Duffield (6) ... 97
Elisa Rogers ... 97
William Jonathan Pearce (6) ... 98
Holly Bray ... 98
Henry Russell (6) ... 99
Sam Richie ... 99
Daisy Parry ... 100

Milverton House Preparatory School, Nuneaton

Tiyana Muchenje (5) ... 100
Sophia Marsh (6) ... 101
Nicole Wood (6) ... 101
Myles Alexander Hellwig (7) ... 102
Milo Peacock (7) ... 102
Lara Underhill (6) ... 103
Grace Knight (7) ... 103
Georgie Samuel Richardson (7) ... 104
Erin Elliott (7) ... 104
Shaan Rai (6) ... 105
Ria Sanghera (6) ... 105
Oskar Metcalfe (6) ... 106
Nomonde Matida Musoko (6) ... 106
Nishita Srinivas (5) ... 107
Mya Jade Kirkbride (6) ... 107
Ibrahim Ahmad (6) ... 108
Alyx Bakewell-Beards (6) ... 108

Megan Cook (7) 109
Mya Khela (7) 109
Ewan Robert Pearce (7) 110

Summerhill Infant School, Bristol

Georgie Leigh Goldswain (5) 110
Catherine Perkins (6) 111
Kian Thomas Maggs (6) 111
Naila Rouf 112
Ella Heaton (6) 112

Tremoilet VCP, Carmarthen

Paulina Wojciechowska (5) 113
Sion Bevan 113
Corey William Mayes (7) 114
Paige Capp 114
Tomos Davies 115
William Sankey 115

The Poems

Sense POETRY – Across The Globe

The Earth

Have you ever seen sweet little birds
gliding slowly with their delicate wings
spread out in the deep blue skies?

Have you ever heard tiny little raindrops
falling and sliding off the slippery rooftops?

Have you ever smelt the beautiful roses
swaying gently in the cool breeze?

Have you ever tasted the lovely ripe apples
on the green, leafy trees?

Have you ever felt a smooth, soft, silky leaf
falling off the big trees?

Mother Earth is so kind
that it sometimes amazes my mind.

Arjun Sawant (7)

On The Way To School

On the way to school,
I see Mike, riding a bike.

On the way to school,
I hear talking and Mike walking.

On the way to school,
I touch the door and Mike's claw.

On the way to school,
I can smell flowers from Mike's tower.

On the way to school,
I can taste tea and Mike tastes wee!

Umamah Batool Hussain (5)

Chocolate

I can see brown wood
I can smell a beautiful smell
I can touch some triangle bars
I can taste the tip of the bars
Yum, yum, yum
What can it be?
It is chocolate!

Vinuga Perera (5)

My Food Dream

One day I lay down on the meadow.
I looked at the blue sky and I began to dream:
'What a shame that the clouds are not made of
vanilla cream...
And those pink -
Are not a raspberry drink...
And those gold and fluffy -
Are not my mum's favourite coffee...
And it's a shame that the sky
Isn't a big, yummy apple pie...
The world would be so beautiful!
I would just lay, like I'm doing now.
I would take my hand high up to the sky and somehow
I would eat those clouds... and eat... and eat...'

Natalia Tyl (5)

Sense POETRY – Across The Globe

The Man Of Senses

A man did not have any eyesight
He smelled his way around
Once he smelled some bubblegum
That landed on the ground.

He licked the ground for the bubblegum
But he could only taste rubber from cars
He felt disgusted and embarrassed
So he wished he could go to Mars.

Then he touched something smooth
And he began to rub it hard
It was a stinky, smelly, shiny boot
From a Buckingham Palace guard.

He heard the thump, thump, thump
Of lots of palace guards
He felt that he was frozen in fear
With all that noise in his ear.

This poor old man used his sniffer
To sniff around the town
He was feeling very tired you see
And he was feeling a little down.

He caught a bus to take him home
So he could go to bed
He had to feel to open the door
Or he would have bumped his head!

Fred Patterson (7)

Miracles

Miracles are all around,
high in the sky and down on the ground
Flowers are miracles, how do they grow?
They come out in the sun and hide in the snow
The sun, the rain, the moon and stars
are all like planets, like Planet Mars
Rainbows are magic, rainbows are bright,
with all the pretty colours like a magical kite
I am a miracle, so are you,
just like my baby sister, Annabella-boo.

Mia Page (6)

My Favourites

My favourite animal is a hippo
I can see it through my window.
I can hear the birds too,
And I watched them as off they flew.

My favourite food are pancakes,
I run down the stairs and mum says, 'Stop making earthquakes!'
Hippos make them as well,
Even louder than my school bell.

My favourite feeling,
Even though it has no meaning,
May have the greatest touch,
But to others it may not mean much.

My favourite smell,
Is one I can never tell.
It's something that tastes like Heaven,
You're just going to have to wait until I'm eleven.

Kassian Rus (6)

Lemon

Yellow, sour, green
As sour as a lollipop
Yellow like the sunshine
The sour, soft, slippy, smooth, shiny, sweet and squeezy lemon is like a firework.

Lemons and limes
Like clementines
The sweet heat makes my heart beat
Like a drum

As cool as an icy waterfall and,
As slippy as an iceberg
Sour
Sour
'Argh!' Sourly sour!

Maariyah Maravia (6)

My Family

Lovely, lovely, lovely
My mummy looks so lovely
Lovely, lovely, lovely
My daddy sounds lovely
I have a little sister Anvi
Who is a sweet little cutie
She runs fast in the house
Like a little Minnie Mouse
She loves to eat cookies
And dance the boogie-woogie
Lovely, lovely, lovely
I love my super family.

Dhriti Manjunath (5)

The Senses Of Love

I remember my Grandpa How who is now living above the clouds.
I remember smelling his peppermint sweet breath, holding me for a cuddle, especially when I
felt sad and blue.
I remember I loved hearing the stories of him, when he was very young.
I remember tasting his home-made pies, when I came home from school.
I remember when we went for walks, he pointed out at the trains zooming back and forth.
I remember hearing the drilling and humming noises coming from a building site.
Grandpa How pointed out to me, he used to work there before.
I remember playing football in the garden one summer's day.
I accidentally broke one of the kitchen windowpanes. *Crack!*
This made house-proud Grandma very cross.
My Grandpa How took the full blame.

Every night I look above at the stars in front of me.
I just want to say in my prayers, I love you and
miss you lots.
I wish you goodnight.
Thank you for the happy times we shared together, all the years ago.

Nathan Peter Lee (6)

An Off-Road Car

An off-road car sounds like a roaring 5.7 litre V8 Hemi engine.
An off-road car feels like a bouncy, bumpy roller coaster.
An off-road car smells like a yummy sandwich for a picnic.
An off-road car tastes like crunchy sand.
An off-road car looks boxy with massive muddy wheels.

Elias Taher (5)

Lady Fingers And Potato Curry

I hear a crackle and pop
I feel a sticky and slippery finger stroking my
hand delicately
I see tall elegant ladies twirling and whirling in a fiery circle, flaming in a
bonfire
I smell mouth-watering, spicy and hot perfume drifting dreamily towards me
I taste an explosion of flavours like sour,
bitter and salty
Oh what a lovely curry!

Kajal Patel (6)

Ice

I can hear the crunch, crunch of the frozen ice.
I can see birds tweeting, stepping in the frozen grass.
I can touch ice that's sparkling.
I can taste frozen air.
I can touch ice glittering. The ice is like diamonds.
I can see sparkly icicles in the distance.
I can touch sparkly icy leaves.
I can hear the sound of the wind.
I can touch icicles on the trees sparkling
in the sunlight.

Olivia Thorpe (5)
Alderbury & West Grimstead CE VA School, Salisbury

Ice

I can see ice on trees.
I can hear snowstorms.
I can see a frozen pond.
I can hear rustling trees.
I can see deep snow.
It is winter.
I can hear tweeting birds.
I can see clouds.
I can see no leaves on trees.
I can hear frozen trees.
I can see slidy ice
I can touch snow.
I can taste cold weather.
I can smell foxes.
I can see snowflakes.
I can see an owl.
I can see holly.
I can see shiny ice, it is cold.
I can see snow falling from the sky.

Emily Linton (5)
Alderbury & West Grimstead CE VA School, Salisbury

Winter

I can see white, beautiful, sparkly ice.
I can hear crunchy, cracking ice.
I can smell cold, fresh, icy air.
I can touch cold, wintry, icy plants and leaves.
I can taste cold fresh air.

Jayden Moody (5), Ryan King (6),Freya, Poppy, Oscar, Max, Amber & Greg
Alderbury & West Grimstead CE VA School, Salisbury

Pit Pat Parrot

Pit Pat Parrot likes eating worms.
It smells of meat.
Pit Pat Parrot might nip you.
It sounds like a bird.
Pit Pat Parrot is yellow and orange.

Yusuf Aden (5)
Assunnah Primary School, London

Silly Old Banana

Silly, silly, silly old banana.
It looks like a yellow crescent.
It tastes delicious.
It feels soft.
It smells very strong.
It sounds like chewing.
Silly, silly, silly old banana.

Tasneem Jama (6)
Assunnah Primary School, London

My Rabbit

My rabbit is cute.
She plays all the time.
She is whitish and blackish.
She crunches and munches.
She feels so soft.
My rabbit is cute.

Riham Mubarak (5)
Assunnah Primary School, London

Silly Bananas

Bananas, bananas.
How silly you are!
First you are green.
You smell so nice.
I really like the way you feel.
But really, you sometimes trick us by going off!

Nusayba Nsubuga (6)
Assunnah Primary School, London

Lions

How scary they are!
A lion growls like a panther.
A lion roars like a dinosaur.
A lion makes crunching noises like a horse.
A lion snores like a dinosaur.
A lion has a sunset-yellow mane.
The mane looks just like the sun!

Mohamed Amin Mahmoud (5)
Assunnah Primary School, London

Cuddly Cow

Cuddly cow.
It looks like a zebra.
Black and white.
It feels tickly.
It crunches when it eats straw.
My cuddly cow moos.
My cuddly cow snores.

Mazin Abbas (6)
Assunnah Primary School, London

Parrots

Oh parrot, get me tea!
My parrot is funny.
What a funny parrot.
It smells like worms
Because it eats worms!
Some parrots are green.
Some are blue.
Oh parrot, get me tea!

Fardowsa Abdikadir (5)
Assunnah Primary School, London

Pizza

Pizza tastes like a warm piece of melting cheese.
Pizza looks like a rocket zooming off to space.
Pizza smells like a nice thing.
Pizza feels like a bumpy hill.
Pizza sounds like a yummy thing to eat.
If I don't get some I will scream!

Subhan Qasimi (6)
Avonmore Primary School, London

Strawberries

Strawberries taste sweet and juicy.
Strawberries smell like marshmallows with chocolate.
Strawberries feel rough and a little bit hairy.
Strawberries sound chewy when you bite them.
Strawberries look tiny, like red and green apples.

Angelina Tarabay (6)
Avonmore Primary School, London

Ice Cream

Ice cream tastes delicious like chocolate melting
in my mouth.
Ice cream smells sweet and delicious.
Ice cream feels cold and soft like mountains.
Ice cream sounds squishy when falling off the cone.
Ice cream looks yummy and it makes me want to eat some now!

Anna Casali (7)
Avonmore Primary School, London

Apple Pie

Apple pie smells like warm apples cooking.
Apple pie feels crunchy and warm.
Apple pie looks bumpy and steamy.
Apple pie tastes like sweet apples and yummy pastry.
Apple pie sounds like good times at home.

Auriana Barboza (6)
Avonmore Primary School, London

Chocolate

When I taste chocolate it makes me want to move and worm.
When I smell chocolate it smells like Heaven.
When I see chocolate it makes me hungry.
When I touch chocolate it melts so quick.
When I hear chocolate it makes me happy.

Daniel O'Mahony (6)
Avonmore Primary School, London

Burgers

Burgers taste like melting cheese on toast.
Burgers look like a piece of sun.
Burgers sound like children cheering.
Burgers feel like a bouncy ball.
Burgers smell like lunchtime.
If I don't get some I may cry!

Dobroslav Kiselev (6)
Avonmore Primary School, London

Oranges

Oranges taste like juicy fruit.
Oranges look like tiny orange tennis balls.
Oranges sound like waterfalls falling.
Oranges feel like bumpy trees.
Oranges smell sweet and sour.

Elizabete Kuduma (6)
Avonmore Primary School, London

Turkey

Turkey smells like my roast dinners.
Turkey feels warm and smooth in my mouth.
Turkey tastes yummy when Mummy makes it.
Turkey looks like the moon in the sky.
Turkey sounds like lots of giggles in the kitchen.

Forozan Azizi (6)
Avonmore Primary School, London

Steak Pie

My steak pie looks like a giant white box.
My steak pie smells like a box of chocolates.
My steak pie tastes hot and delicious.
My steak pie sounds like a crunchy apple.
My steak pie feels really hot and crunchy in my mouth.

Isla Shaw (7)
Avonmore Primary School, London

Raspberries

Raspberries taste like delicious cream.
Raspberries look like a pink, juicy dream.
Raspberries feel like a teddy I've seen.
Raspberries smell like a sour queen.
Raspberries sound like a squeaky bird in the sky.
If I do not get some I will die!

Jasmin Zielinska (6)
Avonmore Primary School, London

Ice Cream

Ice cream tastes like a juicy orange.
Ice cream looks like the sun when it's scooped.
Ice cream sounds like stepping on ice.
Ice cream feels like soft, cold snow.
Ice cream smells like freshly picked strawberries.

Lana Jaukovic (6)
Avonmore Primary School, London

Lasagne

Lasagne looks like orange and white jelly.
Lasagne smells like sweet cake.
Lasagne tastes like fresh sweetcorn.
Lasagne feels squishy like a huge burger.
Lasagne sounds like good times in my house.

Mattewos Zelalem (7)
Avonmore Primary School, London

Pizza

Pizza looks like a flying rocket whooshing into space.
Pizza tastes like cheese melting in my mouth.
Pizza feels rough when I pick it up.
Pizza smells like melting cheese.
Pizza sounds crunchy when I eat it.

Mosab Khalid Abdullahi (7)
Avonmore Primary School, London

Chocolate Cake

Chocolate cake tastes bitter and sweet.
Chocolate cake sounds crunchy like biscuits
when I eat it.
Chocolate cake looks like a mountain of chocolate.
Chocolate cake feels exciting when I eat it.
Chocolate cake smells delicious like a chocolate bath.

Noor Kazim (7)
Avonmore Primary School, London

Chicken Curry And Rice

Chicken curry and rice tastes so good like happiness to me.
Chicken curry and rice smells like my gran's kitchen.
Chicken curry and rice sounds exciting when it's bubbling on the stove.
Chicken curry and rice feels hot and steamy.
Chicken curry and rice looks yummy when I'm waiting for it to cook.
I'm sure you'd love it too!

Pearl Ida (6)
Avonmore Primary School, London

Oranges

Oranges taste sour and sugary.
Oranges look like a meteor travelling from Jupiter.
Oranges smell like sweet sugar.
Oranges feel like cold mashed potato.
Oranges sound like a volcano erupting.

Riley Phillpot-Power (6)
Avonmore Primary School, London

Sausages

Sausages taste delicious.
Sausages smell yummy.
Sausages feel hot to touch.
Sausages look like brown rolls.
Sausages sound quiet and soft.

Ronny Totraku (6)
Avonmore Primary School, London

Wintertime

Red and brown robins pecking around.
What can you hear? Crunchy leaves.
The Christmas cake smells.
You can see snowflakes falling to the ground.
You can eat delicious cake.
You can feel snowflakes falling.

Henry McDonald (6)
Bembridge CE Primary School, Bembridge

Winter Snowman

Children shouting and catching the snowflakes.
See the icicles on the roof.
The smell of hot chocolate in my mug.
The lovely taste of my Christmas dinner.
I can catch the cold, falling snowflakes.

Gabriel Ellingson (5)
Bembridge CE Primary School, Bembridge

Autumn

I can smell things in the breeze.
You can see lovely, sparkly things with your eyes.
We have ears to hear the leaves.
I use my mouth to eat the lovely marshmallows.

Molly Tattersall (5)
Bembridge CE Primary School, Bembridge

Winter Time Is Here

You can see robins in the trees.
Rolling snowballs is cold on your hands.
The smell of hot chocolate is drifting outside.
I like to drink hot, steaming chocolate.
You can hear robins chirping.

Joshua Young (5)
Bembridge CE Primary School, Bembridge

Cold Winter Days

I can touch the snow falling down.
I can see the Christmas tree in the house.
I can taste the hot chocolate in the mug.
I can hear the robins pecking around.
I can smell the Christmas cake drifting through the air.

Ellis Yardley (5)
Bembridge CE Primary School, Bembridge

Autumn Time

We can taste hot chocolate in the autumn.
We can touch the trees and leaves.
We can smell the yummy marshmallows.
We can hear crunchy leaves.
We can see some bare trees.

Mia Cutting (5)
Bembridge CE Primary School, Bembridge

Winter

I can taste hot chocolate.
I can see snow drifting down.
I can hold melting snow.
I can see icicles hanging from my roof.
I can smell the Christmas cake.

Amelia Dutch (6)
Bembridge CE Primary School, Bembridge

In Winter

In winter we can have hot chocolate.
In winter robins are pecking around for food.
The leaves fall down to the ground when
the trees shake.
Leaves are crunchy when you walk on them.
The lovely smell of Christmas cakes.

Max Williams (6)
Bembridge CE Primary School, Bembridge

Winter Days

Winter days are cold.
A steaming hot chocolate.
We can hear the animals crawling around.
You can touch the soft snow.
You can see a snowman being built.
You can smell Christmas cakes cooking.

Ebon Huxley Noall (6)
Bembridge CE Primary School, Bembridge

In Autumn

In autumn I can hear the leaves rustling on the trees.
I can touch the prickly conkers on the floor.
I can see the red leaves falling off the trees.
I can smell hot chocolate in the breeze.
I can taste the cold.

Dylan Wightwick (6)
Bembridge CE Primary School, Bembridge

Winter Is Here

We can see robins.
We can taste hot chocolate.
The wind howls.
We can touch the snow.
We can smell lots of things like mashed potato.

Charlie Michael Duggan (5)
Bembridge CE Primary School, Bembridge

What We Do In Autumn

We can see leaves drifting.
We can taste sweet, delicious marshmallows.
We can smell lots of things in autumn.
We can hear crunching and crumbling leaves
on the ground.
We can feel spiky conkers.

Aoife Bradley (6)
Bembridge CE Primary School, Bembridge

Autumn Leaves

Rustling, crunching leaves falling down.
We can smell smoke steaming from the bonfire.
We can see pretty fireworks.
We can taste a lovely mug of hot chocolate.
We can touch prickly conkers.

Jessica Taylor (6)
Bembridge CE Primary School, Bembridge

Autumn Goes Past

In autumn the golden, red and yellow leaves are falling off the trees.
I can smell chocolate chip biscuits
drifting through the air.
I can feel the round, prickly conkers
lying on the ground.
I like to taste the coldness of the air.
I can hear the crunchy leaves.

Tani Brooks (6)
Bembridge CE Primary School, Bembridge

The Two-Headed Dragon

A two-headed dragon smells like rotten fish flesh.
A two-headed dragon feels scaly, spiky,
pointy and prickly.
A two-headed dragon looks mean and terrifying.
A two-headed dragon tastes like a salty shark.
A two-headed dragon sounds like a windy pig.

Isla Young (7)
Crown Wood Primary School, Bracknell

The Two-Headed Dragon!

The two-headed dragon looks like a terrifying,
fire-breathing lizard.
The two-headed dragon feels like spiky, rough rocks crashing down the mountain.
The two-headed dragon smells like disgusting dinosaur dung.
The two-headed dragon sounds like a drum being banged on by a Viking.
The two-headed dragon tastes like rotten lion meat.

Bryony Thompson (6)
Crown Wood Primary School, Bracknell

My Dragon Poem

A dragon tastes like the blood of a knight.
A dragon smells like rotting cabbage.
A dragon sounds like giant footsteps.
A dragon looks like red melting lava coming from a big volcano.

Frankie Garner (6)
Crown Wood Primary School, Bracknell

My Dragon Poem

My dragon sounds like dangerous thunderstorms in the night sky.
My dragon looks like a fierce flying monster.
My dragon smells like burning houses.
My dragon tastes like a burning hot bonfire.
My dragon feels like bumpy, hard rocks.

Keira Lee (7)
Crown Wood Primary School, Bracknell

My Dragon Poem

A dragon tastes like leather boots
that have been worn.
A dragon sounds like two tigers about to fight.
A dragon feels as scaly as fish scales.
A dragon looks like a lion without a mane.
A dragon smells like a human who hasn't had
a bath in ages!

Freya Brooks (7)
Crown Wood Primary School, Bracknell

A Dragon

A dragon sounds like burning lava that has
just exploded.
A dragon looks like a terrifying T-rex.
A dragon tastes like an old knight's armour.
A dragon feels like scaly, rotting fish flesh.
A dragon smells like the smelly moat of a big castle.

Harley Fordham (6)
Crown Wood Primary School, Bracknell

A Dragon Poem

A dragon sounds like deadly scratching.
A dragon's mouth looks like an erupting volcano.
A dragon tastes like burning ham.
A dragon smells like burning fire lava.
A dragon feels like a huge burning volcano.

Jamie Newstead (7)
Crown Wood Primary School, Bracknell

A Dragon Poem

A dragon tastes like rotten fish flesh
left in the sun for years.
A dragon looks like a burning, exploding volcano, shooting out lava and rocks.
A dragon feels like scaly scales.
A dragon smells like rotting fish.
A dragon sounds like a huge thunderstorm.

Jayden Denzil Bradbury (6)
Crown Wood Primary School, Bracknell

Pancakes

The batter makes me hungry.
Pancakes taste sweet and sour and they feel sticky.
They look yummy scrummy.
I can hear the popping and sizzling.
Suddenly, they land on me!

Olivia Stafford-Bennett (6)
Cullingworth Village Primary School, Bradford

Pancakes

Pancakes, pancakes, they are sweet.
Pancakes, pancakes, hear the sizzle.
Pancakes, pancakes, they smell of chocolate.
Pancakes, pancakes, they feel soft.

Macsen Morris (5)
Cullingworth Village Primary School, Bradford

Pancakes

Pancakes
Pop go the pancakes.
I can hear the sizzling pancakes in the pan.
Now in my tummy, they were yummy!
They tasted like chocolate and smelt so sweet.

Lyla Illingworth (5)
Cullingworth Village Primary School, Bradford

Pancakes

I can smell the pancakes.
I hear the sizzling pancakes in the pan.
They taste like chocolate.
They feel squishy.
They look like a golden circle.

Lucy Walker (5)
Cullingworth Village Primary School, Bradford

Pancakes

The smell is yummy.
Its taste is funny,
I can hear a sizzle in the pan.
I can see the colour of gold.
I can feel the gooey and sticky pancake as I put it in my mouth.

Lily Diamond (6)
Cullingworth Village Primary School, Bradford

Pancakes

The pancakes smell delicious.
The pancakes are good to eat.
The pancakes are hot to touch.
The pancakes are good to eat.
The pancakes are yummy.

Finlay Gardner (5)
Cullingworth Village Primary School, Bradford

Pancakes

Pancakes taste like sweets.
Pop and *sizzle* went the pancakes.
Flip went the pancakes.
Flip, flip, flip.

Pancakes were on the ceiling and one
dripping down the wall.
I could smell the golden, crisp pancake and taste the sweet and sour.
Flip, flip, flip.

Ava-Jean McTurk (5)
Cullingworth Village Primary School, Bradford

Pancakes

The pancake tastes like jam.
I can hear the sizzling in the pan.
It is yummy in my tummy.
I can see the pancake sizzling in the pan.

Angelina Gloire Rumwagira (5)
Cullingworth Village Primary School, Bradford

Pancakes

The pancake race
Pancakes are the yummiest.
I love them.
Go on pancakes, you can win the pancake race.
Flip and toss in the air.
Oh they smell so sugary.

Madison Parkinson (6)
Cullingworth Village Primary School, Bradford

Pancake Day

I hear pancakes buzzing in the pan like a bumblebee.
I'm smelling, I'm hearing and I'm seeing yummy pancakes everywhere.
I flip them and eat them all up.

Zoey Lauren Ross (6)
Cullingworth Village Primary School, Bradford

Pancake Day

I can hear popping and banging and sizzling
all day long.
The pancakes smell like sugar syrup.
They feel squishy, tasty and yummy
with a golden crisp.

Isabelle Holdsworth (5)
Cullingworth Village Primary School, Bradford

Pancakes

It smells delicious.
I can hear it pop.
It tastes hot.
I can see it sizzling.

Jack Bennett (6)
Cullingworth Village Primary School, Bradford

My School

In my school I can smell lovely lunch.
In my school I can taste delicious lunch.
In my school I can hear straight tables being placed down.
In my school I can touch the hard floor.
In my school I can see school children working hard in English.

Dylan Cooper (7)
Gatten And Lake Primary School, Shanklin

My School

In my school I can smell lovely dinner and honey.
In my school I can taste fresh air.
In my school I can hear loud people, seagulls cheeping, moving chairs and noisy people.
In my school I can touch fresh air.
In my school I can see bare trees, chairs and instruments.

Holly Paxton-Ford (6)
Gatten And Lake Primary School, Shanklin

Untitled

The zoo smells like animals.
The zoo tastes like juice.
The zoo sounds like tigers.
The zoo feels like lunch.
The zoo looks like animals.

Rubi Anne Harper (6)
Gatten And Lake Primary School, Shanklin

The Zoo

The zoo smells like lunch
The zoo tastes like strawberries
The zoo looks like tigers.

Michael Manning (5)
Gatten And Lake Primary School, Shanklin

Untitled

The zoo smells like chips
The zoo tastes like lava
The zoo sounds like a farm
The zoo feels like a sandwich
The zoo looks like muddy boots.

Nicole Amy Clio Beale (6)
Gatten And Lake Primary School, Shanklin

Untitled

The zoo smells like dirt
The zoo tastes like Twirls
The zoo sounds like lions
The zoo looks like the coach.

Jayden Russell
Gatten And Lake Primary School, Shanklin

Untitled

The zoo smells like grass and mud
The zoo tastes like apple and biscuit
The zoo sounds like orange lemurs
The zoo feels like lunch
The zoo looks like Tracy.

Rosie Tayler (6)
Gatten And Lake Primary School, Shanklin

Untitled

The zoo smells like coffee
The zoo sounds like a roaring lion
The zoo looks like Tracy
The zoo tastes like milk
The zoo feels like lunch.

Diana Madaras
Gatten And Lake Primary School, Shanklin

Untitled

The zoo smells like animals
The zoo tastes like water
The zoo sounds like a lion
The zoo feels like lunch
The zoo looks like a zoo.

Reggie-Joe Brown (6)
Gatten And Lake Primary School, Shanklin

The Zoo

The zoo smells like lunch and juice
The zoo tastes like sandwiches and a KitKat
The zoo sounds like Casper the lion
The zoo feels like lunch and drinks
The zoo looks like the zoo.

Vinnie Ray Dennis (6)
Gatten And Lake Primary School, Shanklin

The Zoo

The zoo smells like mud
The zoo tastes like an apple
The zoo sounds like monkeys
The zoo looks like a zoo
The zoo smells like lunch.

Enes Yigit Korkmaz
Gatten And Lake Primary School, Shanklin

The Zoo Sense

The zoo smells like lunch
The zoo tastes like rolls
The zoo sounds like a lion
The zoo feels like lunch
The zoo looks like a zoo.

Harry English
Gatten And Lake Primary School, Shanklin

The Zoo

The zoo smells like coffee,
The zoo tastes like an apple,
The zoo sounds like birds,
The zoo feels like drinks,
The zoo looks like animals.

Olivia Bird
Gatten And Lake Primary School, Shanklin

Sense POETRY – Across The Globe

My School

In my school I can hear noisy children.
I can hear trees swishing.
I can smell lovely dinner.
I can smell Mrs Millis's perfume.
I can touch a glittery stone wall.
I can touch Julia's long, soft hair.

Charlotte Emily Page (6)
Gatten And Lake Primary School, Shanklin

My School

In my school I can smell lunch.
In my school I can taste fresh air.
In my school I can hear birds tweeting.
In my school I can touch books.
In my school I can see houses.

Chloe Elizabeth Welsh (6)
Gatten And Lake Primary School, Shanklin

My School

In my school I can smell lovely dinner.
In my school I can taste warm air.
In my school I can hear tables getting moved.
In my school I can touch a smooth chair.
In my school I can see Miss Cox talking.

Grace Robinson (7)
Gatten And Lake Primary School, Shanklin

My School

In my school I can hear children screaming.
In my school I can touch fluffy clothes.
In my school I can see my lovely friends.
In my school I can smell yummy lunch.
In my school I can taste tasty dinners.

Julia Blok (6)
Gatten And Lake Primary School, Shanklin

My School

In my school I can smell yummy orange
In my school I can taste delicious lunch
In my school I can hear scraping pencils
In my school I can feel a hard table
In my school I can see people writing nicely.

Matthew Moralee (6)
Gatten And Lake Primary School, Shanklin

Untitled

I can smell lunch
I can taste Mrs Miller's perfume
I can hear wind
I can feel scooters
I can see Callum.

Ruby Jones (7)
Gatten And Lake Primary School, Shanklin

My School

I can see children playing netball.
I can smell lunch.
I can touch the floor.
I can hear the wind blowing.
I can taste water from the fountain.

Alfie Beeney (7)
Gatten And Lake Primary School, Shanklin

My School

In my school...
I can see working children.
I can hear children chatting.
I can touch the wet bench.
I can smell delicious food.
I can taste frozen air on my lips.

Amber Sheaff (6)
Gatten And Lake Primary School, Shanklin

My School

In my school I hear shouting children.
I smell yummy dinner.
I see Marley.
I feel a bumpy chair.

Aiden Beckley (7)
Gatten And Lake Primary School, Shanklin

My School

In my school I can see people talking.
In my school I can taste the fruit.
In my school I can hear people talking.
In my school I can smell Mrs Miller's perfume.
In my school I can hear people creeping.
In my school I can see people learning.

Jessica Louise Moore (6)
Gatten And Lake Primary School, Shanklin

My School

I can smell a cake.
I can see a bird in the tree.
I touch a chair.
I can hear a bird.
I can see taps.

Marley Samuel Dyer (6)
Gatten And Lake Primary School, Shanklin

My School

In my school I can taste my very lovely, yummy
packed lunch.
In my school I can smell very super delicious school dinners that taste nice.
In my school I can see children who are my friends.
In my school I can touch very exciting
school equipment.
In my school I can hear my brilliant teacher talking.

Matthew Manning (7)
Gatten And Lake Primary School, Shanklin

In School

In my school people laugh.
In my school I can touch a chair.
In my school I see a bird.
In my school I can smell lunch cooking.
In my school I can taste banana.

Cailub Harbour (7)
Gatten And Lake Primary School, Shanklin

My School

In my school I can see lovely teachers.
In my school I can taste cold air.
In my school I can touch a wavy table.
In my school I can smell delicious dinner.
In my school I can hear loud children.

Phoebe Arnold (7)
Gatten And Lake Primary School, Shanklin

Senses Poem

I can see the big board
I can feel a plastic chair
I can smell the fresh air.

Qaid Al Aswad (6)
Harlesden Primary School, London

Senses Poem

I can hear birds twitting
I can see a colourful staircase
I can taste yummy cake
I can feel a soft carpet.

Genius Cowans (5)
Harlesden Primary School, London

Senses Poem

I can see green plants
I can hear loud wind
I can smell hot food
I can feel a blue window
I can taste yummy pasta
I can feel toys.

Nuhad Hasan Khan (5)
Harlesden Primary School, London

Senses Poem

I can taste a yummy banana
I can feel a hard wall
I can see blonde people
I can hear noisy people
I can smell white car smoke.

Mijuwada Parambil (6)
Harlesden Primary School, London

Lollipops

Lollipops look like sparkling fireworks in the sky.
Lollipops smell like caramel.
Lollipops taste like fruity sweets.
Lollipops feel hard like rock.
Lollipops sound like a merry-go-round.

Ellie Louden (8)
Heriot Primary School, Paisley

Lollipops

Lollipops look like bright fireworks.
Lollipops smell like sweet apples and
strong, minty toothpaste.
Lollipops taste like colourful, fizzy rainbow drops and sugary candyfloss.
Lollipops feel smooth like desks to work on.
Lollipops sound like my favourite song and
happiness all around.

Ewan Murray (7)
Heriot Primary School, Paisley

Lollipops

Lollipops look like a dream come true, they are so fantastic like balloons.
Lollipops smell like lovely, delicious fruity candy.
Lollipops taste like strong, fizzy candy, such real and good things.
Lollipops feel hard like a big candy brick on a wall.
Lollipops sound like a big crowd laughing at something funny.

Ewan Jamieson (7)
Heriot Primary School, Paisley

Lollipops

Lollipops look like an amazing, colourful
dream come true
Lollipops smell like cherries and berries exploding over a sugary rainbow
Lollipops taste like fruity raindrops dropping from the beautiful sky
Lollipops feel sticky like chewing gum stuck to the bottom of my shoe
Lollipops sound like a merry-go-round, going round and round and singing a happy tune.

Hannah McCallum (7)
Heriot Primary School, Paisley

Lollipops

Lollipops look like bright shooting stars that go flying across the dark purple sky.
Lollipops smell like sweet cherries and strawberries.
Lollipops taste like colourful, fizzy rainbow drops and fresh apples.
Lollipops feel smooth like colourful silk.
Lollipops sound like happy dolphins.

Eva Lousie Slimmon (7)
Heriot Primary School, Paisley

Lollipops

Lollipops look like a dream come true.
Lollipops smell like oranges and apples.
Lollipops taste like your tongue is exploding.
Lollipops feel smooth like a brick.
Lollipops sound like a merry-go-round.

Riley Meechan (7)
Heriot Primary School, Paisley

Sense POETRY – Across The Globe

Lollipops

Lollipops look like a lovely, sour, yummy strawberry.
Lollipops smell like rainbows, apples
and gummy bears.
Lollipops taste like a delicious fizzy, caramel,
fruity candyfloss.
Lollipops feel sticky like pollen in a flower.
Lollipops sound like children's laughter and playing my favourite song.

Sophie Karen Help (8)
Heriot Primary School, Paisley

Lollipops

Lollipops look like swirling, curling fireworks in the sky, banging and bashing together.
Lollipops smell like a sweet banana, berries, cherries and apples.
Lollipops taste like delicious, fruity, sugary,
minty toothpaste.
Lollipops feel sticky like goo in my Gooey Louie game.
Lollipops sound like a happy breeze in the summer.

Morgan Gallacher (7)
Heriot Primary School, Paisley

Lollipops

Lollipops look like colourful fireworks bashing together in the sky.
Lollipops smell like fruity cherries, berries and apples.
Lollipops taste like strawberry candyfloss and fizzy rainbow drops.
Lollipops feel smooth like wonderful flowers deep down in the grass.
Lollipops sound like happy dolphins singing a wonderful tune.

Keira Abbie Quinn (7)
Heriot Primary School, Paisley

Lollipops

Lollipops look like fireworks glowing in the
colourful, bright sky.
Lollipops smell like colourful gummy bears that explode in my mouth.
Lollipops taste like lovely fizzy rainbow drops, candyfloss, banana, apple
and tangy orange.
Lollipops feel sticky like a piece of gooey Play-Doh.
Lollipops sound like big dolphins playing in the
deep blue sea.

Richard McKnight (8)
Heriot Primary School, Paisley

Lollipops

Lollipops look like colourful fireworks in the sky.
Lollipops smell like fizzy, colourful lemons.
Lollipops taste like minty, gummy, fruity rainbows.
Lollipops feel hard like big rocks in the mountains.
Lollipops sound like happy children.

Marcus Issac (7)
Heriot Primary School, Paisley

Lollipops

Lollipops look like great, big, colourful fireworks dancing in the sky.
Lollipops smell like tangy gummy bears with a
coating of fruit.
Lollipops taste like delicious, sugary, sour, colourful fruit in your hand.
Lollipops feel sticky like the goo in the nearby sewer
in the ground.
Lollipops sound like children laughing in a fairground and having lots of fun.

Jamie Hunter (7)
Heriot Primary School, Paisley

Lollipops

Lollipops look like sparkling fireworks in the sky.
Lollipops smell like raspberry and apple delight.
Lollipops taste like swirling rainbow delight.
Lollipops feel smooth like colourful fabric.
Lollipops sound like happy dolphins in the ocean.

Hayden Hodgkinson (8)
Heriot Primary School, Paisley

Lollipops

Lollipops look like awesome, beautiful fireworks in the colourful sky.
Lollipops smell like lovely cherries and apples that are so sweet they burst in your mouth.
Lollipops taste like fizzy candy drops that are so minty they make your brain explode.
Lollipops feel hard like boulders at the seaside that you throw in the big sea.
Lollipops sound like my happiest tune that I love so much, I stay up all night listening to it.

Jamie McKechnie (7)
Heriot Primary School, Paisley

Sixth Sense

If there was a sixth sense what would it be?
If there was a sixth sense it would apply to
you and me,
There is already taste, touch, sight, smell and hearing,
But I'll think of something with all my might and I will think of it tonight.

Zoe Whitaker
Jumeirah English Speaking School, Dubai

I Love Sweets

When I open the bright red wrapper I can hear the crinkling sounds
The bright pink colour of sweets is shiny like
a disco ball
One sweet smells like a succulent strawberry, it feels squishy when I touch it
When I put the sweet in my mouth I can taste the lovely burst of sweet
sugar
I wish I could eat sweets every day but my teacher
won't let me!

Azarin Jalaei (7)
Jumeirah English Speaking School, Dubai

Hot Chocolate

Hot chocolate swirling in the pan
The tinkling of the stirrer reminding me of Gran
The snowball marshmallows floating on the tan
The steaming soup now needs a fan
But once it is cool enough to drink, the feeling,
oh man!

The marshmallow snowballs go *plop*
Whilst chocolate bubbles do pop
Sweet smell in the air
It's hot so take care
Taste the cool, fluffy whipped cream on top.

Hot chocolate's sweet smell fills the air
Hot chocolate bubbles in the pan
Hot chocolate pouring into my mug
Hot chocolate warming my hands
Hot chocolate dribbles down my throat
Hot chocolate, my favourite treat of all.

Ayanna Sethi (7)
Jumeirah English Speaking School, Dubai

Food

Food is sour, spicy or sweet.
It's very nice and scrumptious to eat.
It smells light or strong.
Sometimes the smell does not last for long.
Food looks tiny, big or huge.
Some feels so sticky you can't move.
You can find food in the north and south.
You can hear it crunch in your mouth.

Shreya Kopuri
Jumeirah English Speaking School, Dubai

A Walk Through The Forest

I can see huge, tall, swaying trees,
Thousands of waving green leaves.

I feel the spongy, damp, thick, soft, green tree moss.
I can hear birds chirping, in the distance a woodpecker working.

I can see rabbit holes under the bushes.
I hear squirrels rustling in the trees,
Collecting nuts for the winter freeze.

I can sense animals everywhere in nests and burrows.

I can smell blackberries fresh and ripe but
I won't pick them because they'll be the forest animals' tea tonight.

I can see wild strawberries like red jewels in a bush.
I can't resist, they taste yummy,
So I fill my tummy.

Asta Maddox (7)
Jumeirah English Speaking School, Dubai

Your poem has been chosen as the best in this book!

The Four Seasons

Winter is white with powdery snow and cold
to the touch.
Children screaming while they
sledge down a hill.

Snow melting in spring, green grass sprouting,
flowers blooming, leaves growing and
animals peeping
out from their habitats, looking for food.

Bright sunshine shining down on a field full of corn,
people lying under the shady trees, trying
to stay away from the heat.

Autumn is happy times when pumpkins grow,
ready to be freshly picked for Halloween.
The red, yellow, brown and orange leaves ready
to be raked.

Winter is white,
Spring is green,
Summer is yellow,
And autumn is a blend of red, orange,
brown and yellow.

Jodyn Foong (6)
Jumeirah English Speaking School, Dubai

The Beach

Waves crashing, waves splashing
Rocks cracking against the water
Crabs snapping across the sand
The morning sand is as cool as a refrigerator
Closer to the shore you feel the movement of the water between your toes
Soft and yellow sand
Dark green seaweed that waves in the water
In the distance big ships sail across the shiny seas
Fresh air with a scent of lemon
Constant smell of salt lingering in the air
Rusty ships sailing through the crashing seas
Clear but salty water stings my mouth.

Thomas Ding
Jumeirah English Speaking School, Dubai

Fruit Fun

I see a pineapple, its top as sharp as knives.
I hear an orange tearing, hissing as quiet as a mouse.
I smell a kiwi as fresh as Refresher sweeties.
I taste a banana as sweet as ice cream.
I touch an apple – soft, round and smooth like a ball.

Isla Jack (5)
Keiss Primary School, Wick

Fruit Salad

I see a banana as yellow as the sun.
I touch a lychee as spiky as a hedgehog.
I taste a kiwi as sour as a lemon.
I taste pomegranate as sweet as candy.
I touch a pineapple as spiky as a hedgehog.

Zoe Mackay (6)
Keiss Primary School, Wick

Fruit Fun

I see a banana as bendy as a smiley face.
I hear an apple crunch like a crocodile snapping.
I smell an orange as tangy as seaweed.
I taste a lemon as sour as a lollipop.
I touch a pineapple as spiky as a hedgehog.

Tyler Campbell (7)
Keiss Primary School, Wick

Fruity Fun

I see an apple as round as a bouncy ball.
I hear an orange peel as hissy as a snake.
I smell a lychee as flowery as the soap in the dentist.
I taste a pomegranate as popping as popping candy.
I touch a pineapple as spiky as a crocodile's back.

Alexander Mackay (6)
Keiss Primary School, Wick

Fruit Fun

I see an apple as green as grass.
I hear a lychee as cracky as a Christmas cracker.
I smell a banana as yellow as the sun.
I taste a lemon as sharp as scissors.
I touch a pineapple as spiky as a cactus.

Aimee Lowe (6)
Keiss Primary School, Wick

Fruit Salad

I see a banana as yellow as the sun.
I hear pineapple leaves as squeaky as a mouse.
I smell a kiwi as fresh as the air outside.
I taste a lychee as sweet as popping candy.
I touch an apple as smooth as new paper.

Ella-May Merry (6)
Keiss Primary School, Wick

Fruit Fun

I see an orange as round as a ball.
I hear a banana peeling, cracking like rocks falling.
I smell a pomegranate as sweet as candy.
I taste a lemon as sour as a lollipop.
I touch a kiwi, hairy like a lion's mane.

Callum Booth (5)
Keiss Primary School, Wick

Fruit Fun

I see an apple as hard as a bone.
I hear a Minion-yellow banana peeling.
I smell a lychee as sweet as a poppy.
I taste a lime as sharp as a knife.
I touch a lychee as spiky as an alligator's back.

Islay Anderson (6)
Keiss Primary School, Wick

Fruity Fun

I see a pomegranate as ruby-red as a jewel.
I hear a banana peeling like bubble wrap popping.
I smell a lemon as new as fresh air.
I taste an orange as sweet as chocolate.
I touch a pineapple as prickly as a porcupine.

Caitlyn Fitzimmons (5)
Keiss Primary School, Wick

Fruit Bowl

I see a lychee as spikey as dinosaur teeth.
I hear an apple crunching like tree branches
in a storm.
I smell a grape as sour as coffee.
I taste a pineapple tickling my lips like tickling fingers.

Loïc Manson (5)
Keiss Primary School, Wick

The Beach

The beach sounds like squeaking seagulls.
The beach feels like bumpy rocks.
The beach looks like wavy sea.
The beach smells like sweet ice cream.
The beach tastes like chocolate ice cream.

Tilly Thorpe
Kingshill Infant School, Ware

The Beach

The beach sounds like loud seagulls.
The beach tastes like cold ice cream.
The beach looks like little rocks.

William Glenister
Kingshill Infant School, Ware

The Park

The park sounds like loud birds tweeting.
The park feels like big metal slides.
The park looks like big blue slides.
The park smells like chocolate ice cream.
The park tastes like chocolate ice cream.

Felix Flanagan
Kingshill Infant School, Ware

The Park

The park sounds like talking.
The park feels like slides.
The park tastes like cold ice cream.
The park smells like cold ice cream.

Zoe Boldick (6)
Kingshill Infant School, Ware

The Beach

The beach sounds like loud seagulls.
The beach smells like sweet ice cream.
The beach feels like tickly sand.
The beach tastes like salty sea.

Poppy Booth
Kingshill Infant School, Ware

The Park

The park smells like pink flowers.
The park looks like round ice cream.
The park sounds like big white birds.
The park feels like hard rocks.

Maisie Draper (5)
Kingshill Infant School, Ware

The Beach

The beach sounds like loud waves.
The beach feels like salty water.
The beach looks like the blue sea.
The beach smells like salty chips.

Callum Glover
Kingshill Infant School, Ware

The Beach

The beach smells like salty fish and chips.
The beach feels like soft sand.
The beach sounds like blue sea.
The beach tastes like cold ice cream.
The beach looks like big rocks.

Isabel-Rose Haldenby (6)
Kingshill Infant School, Ware

The Park

The park sounds like swaying trees.
At the park it smells like ice cream.
At the park are squawking blackbirds.
At the park it feels like a smooth slide.

Chloe Rose Abraham (5)
Kingshill Infant School, Ware

The Park

The park sounds like chattering, happy children.
The park tastes like cold, tasty, strawberry ice cream.
The park smells like cold, spiky leaves.
The park looks like blowing, green grass.
The park feels like smooth, metal bars.

Lottie Hill
Kingshill Infant School, Ware

The Park

The park smells like vanilla ice cream with sprinkles.
The park feels like metal, it is shiny and cold.
The park looks like a queue onto the slide.
The park sounds like children chattering a new song.
The park tastes like wavy wind.

Erin Bellamy (5)
Kingshill Infant School, Ware

The Beach

The beach sounds like huge seagulls.
The beach smells like greasy fish and chips.
The beach looks like blue, deep sea.
The beach tastes like fluffy, big ice cream.
The beach feels like rough sand.

Coby Friedner (6)
Kingshill Infant School, Ware

At The Park

At the park you can hear the children laughing.
At the park you can feel the tree bark.
At the park you can see children playing.
At the park you can smell sweet ice cream.
At the park you can taste flavoured ice cream.

Bow Tierney
Kingshill Infant School, Ware

The Beach

The beach sounds like wavy sea.
The beach feels like bumpy rocks.
The beach smells like salty sea.
The beach looks like orange crabs.
The beach tastes like tasty ice lollies.

Finn O'Neill (6)
Kingshill Infant School, Ware

The Beach

The beach looks like gold coins.
The beach sounds like big waves.
The beach tastes like chocolate ice cream.
The beach smells like fish fingers.
The beach tastes of salt.

Mabel Farrell (5)
Kingshill Infant School, Ware

The Beach

The beach looks like blue sea.
The beach smells like seaweed.
The beach tastes like ice cream.
The beach feels like yellow sand.
The beach sounds like seagulls.

Isabel Hall (6)
Kingshill Infant School, Ware

The Park

The park looks like birds singing.
The park sounds like people screaming.
The park feels like hard wood.
The park smells lovely.
The park tastes like an apple.

Ioan Rhys James (5)
Kingshill Infant School, Ware

The Beach

The beach looks like waves smashing.
The beach sounds like singing seagulls.
The beach feels like soft, smooth sand.
The beach tastes like cold, slippery ice cream.
The beach smells like a picnic.

Morten Tveit (5)
Kingshill Infant School, Ware

The Beach

The beach looks like a big beach.
The beach sounds like a shiny seagull.
The beach feels like soft sand.
The beach smells like green seaweed.
The beach tastes like nice strawberries.

Bethany Lippiatt (6)
Kingshill Infant School, Ware

The Beach

The beach looks like yellow, smooth sand.
The beach tastes like yummy pepperoni pizza.
The beach smells like salty seaweed.
The beach feels like rough rocks.
The beach sounds like seagulls singing.

Harry Samuel (6)
Kingshill Infant School, Ware

The Beach

The beach looks like blue wavy sea.
The beach smells like brown crunchy chocolate.
The beach tastes like yummy cheese and tomato pizza.
The beach sounds like white noisy seagulls.
The beach feels like yellow sand.

Abbey Johnson (5)
Kingshill Infant School, Ware

The Park

The park looks like birds singing.
The park smells like yummy chocolate.
The park sounds like people laughing.
The park feels like brushing leaves.
The park tastes like yummy pizza.

Holly May Kimpton (6)
Kingshill Infant School, Ware

The Park

The park looks like shiny bars.
The park smells like strawberry ice cream.
The park tastes like pizza with mayo.
The park sounds like leaves crunching.
The park feels like muddy, dark trees.

Neave Baker (5)
Kingshill Infant School, Ware

The Beach

The beach looks like big water.
The beach sounds like seagulls.
The beach feels like hard sand.
The beach smells like ice cream.
The beach tastes like salty water.

Evie Grace Crolla (6)
Kingshill Infant School, Ware

The Beach

The beach looks like a sandy beach.
The beach feels like silky skin.
The beach tastes like seaweed.
The beach sounds like swishing waves.
The beach smells like a barbecue.

Erin Bartholomew (5)
Kingshill Infant School, Ware

The Beach

The beach looks like yellow jelly.
The beach sounds like seagulls.
The beach feels like soft sand.
The beach smells like slimy seaweed.
The beach tastes of fish.

Ethan Neighbour (5)
Kingshill Infant School, Ware

The Forest

The forest smells of damp leaves.
The forest sounds like birds.
The forest tastes like pizza.
The forest looks like brown trees.
The forest feels like leaves.

Olly Gumble (6)
Kingshill Infant School, Ware

The Forest

The forest looks like dropping leaves.
The forest sounds like crunchy leaves.
The forest feels like tree trunks.
The forest smells like a picnic.
The forest tastes like a cheese sandwich.

Harry Watson (5)
Kingshill Infant School, Ware

The Forest

The forest smells like Christmas.
The forest looks like wood.
The forest tastes like strawberries.
The forest feels like rough sandpaper.
The forest sounds like swishing trees.

Emily Jay Bourne (5)
Kingshill Infant School, Ware

My Five Senses

I love to see my kind friends.
I love to hear wind whistling.
I love to touch cold snow.
I love to smell chocolatey cookies.
I love to taste delicious spaghetti Bolognese.

Ruby Garside (7)
Leslie Primary School, Glenrothes

My Five Senses

I love to see lightning flashing.
I love to hear Minecraft music.
I love to touch my Lego Ninja sets.
I love to smell pancakes cooking in the oven.
I love to taste scrumptious bubblegum juice.

Josh Taylor (7)
Leslie Primary School, Glenrothes

My Five Senses

I love to see houses.
I love to hear cars beeping.
I love to touch my Xbox controller.
I love to smell hot chocolate.
I love to taste strawberry ice cream.

Joss McKinlay (7)
Leslie Primary School, Glenrothes

My Five Senses

I love to see my gran's cute puppy.
I love to hear huge aeroplanes taking off.
I love to touch ponies in the field.
I love to smell pretty daisies.
I love to taste delicious hot chocolate.

Peyton Gillespie (7)
Leslie Primary School, Glenrothes

Sense POETRY – Across The Globe

My Five Senses

I love to see the crashing waves.
I love to hear the seagulls squawking.
I love to touch giant seashells.
I love to smell pancakes.
I love to taste McDonald's.

Emma McIntyre (7)
Leslie Primary School, Glenrothes

My Five Senses

I love to see buses beeping.
I love to hear seagulls squawking.
I love to touch my dog and bunny.
I love to smell water in the pool.
I love to taste vanilla ice cream.

James Wilson (7)
Leslie Primary School, Glenrothes

My Five Senses

I love to see enormous boats.
I love to hear giant planes and helicopters.
I love to touch my furry tiny dog.
I love to smell yummy fish and chips.
I love to taste mountain dew.

Idris Mowbray (7)
Leslie Primary School, Glenrothes

My Five Senses

I like to see a colourful, pretty rainbow.
I like to hear the loud, noisy wind outside.
I like to touch a beautiful daisy and a white tulip.
I like to smell hot chocolate and
chocolate chip cookies.
I like to taste melted dark chocolate.

Brooke Gibson (7)
Leslie Primary School, Glenrothes

My Five Senses

I love to see cakes rising in the oven and
my pretty mum.
I love to hear popping candy and horses clip-clopping.
I love to touch my sparkling glitter pens
and paintbrushes.
I love to smell hot cocoa in a warm cup.
I love to taste red and white patterned candy canes.

Charley Rutherford Gallacher (7)
Leslie Primary School, Glenrothes

My Five Senses

I love to see my marvellous mum.
I love to hear my evil cat hissing.
I love to touch my little, mucky, cute teddy bear.
I love to smell my dad's best cake in the oven.
I love to taste the best pancakes in the world from
my auntie Kerry.

Connor Blackie (7)
Leslie Primary School, Glenrothes

My Five Senses

I love to see the huge Falkland Hill.
I love to hear big seagulls squawking loudly.
I love to touch my fluffy teddy.
I love to smell tasty sausages.
I love to taste yummy pizza.

Deren Mede (7)
Leslie Primary School, Glenrothes

My Five Senses

I love to see golden trophies.
I love to hear colourful fireworks.
I love to touch a fluffy dog.
I love to smell fizzy Lucozade.
I love to taste carbonara and hot chocolate.

Cole Senkel (7)
Leslie Primary School, Glenrothes

My Five Senses

I love to see a beautiful flower growing.
I love to hear the sound of loud, tweeting birds
I love to taste sweet, juicy strawberries.
I love to touch soft, fluffy teddies.
I love to smell delicious hot dogs.

Mason Ross (6)
Leslie Primary School, Glenrothes

My Five Senses

I love to smell the wonderful flowers.
I love to hear my cute dog bark.
I love to touch my cuddly teddy bears.
I love to see beautiful Mrs Fraser.
I love to taste tasty chocolate cake.

Murron Pratt (6)
Leslie Primary School, Glenrothes

My Five Senses

I love to hear my brother playing with cars.
I love to see Easter eggs.
I love to smell daisies.
I love to touch my cousin's hair.
I love to taste yellow bananas.

Mikolaj Krzysztof Zubowicz (6)
Leslie Primary School, Glenrothes

My Five Senses

I love to hear my dog bark because it's lovely.
I love to see my wonderful mum and dad.
I love to smell the fresh air.
I love to touch the old oak tree.
I love to taste squidgy chocolate cake.

Lucy Dryburgh (6)
Leslie Primary School, Glenrothes

My Five Senses

I love to see my brother play.
I love to hear my mum and dad.
I love to touch my mum.
I love to smell tasty ice cream.
I love to taste sticky cake.

Libby Milne (6)
Leslie Primary School, Glenrothes

My Five Senses

I love to see my good, cuddly dog.
I love to hear my dog bark so loud.
I love to smell delicious chocolate cake in the oven.
I love to touch my nice toes.
I love to taste yummy apples.

Keira Simpson (6)
Leslie Primary School, Glenrothes

My Five Senses

I love to see tall trees.
I love to hear Benji bark.
I love to touch my cheeky dog.
I love to smell sweet Weetabix.
I love to taste chocolate cake.

Josh Gorrie (6)
Leslie Primary School, Glenrothes

My Five Senses

I love to see big seagulls.
I love to hear Ava.
I love to smell cake.
I love to taste macaroni.
I love to touch my soft toys.

Freya Jane Stewart (6)
Leslie Primary School, Glenrothes

Sense POETRY – Across The Globe

My Five Senses

I love to hear lovely birds tweet.
I love to see Roxy and Hop playing together.
I love to smell chocolate cake.
I love to touch cold glass.
I love to taste sticky sweets.

Charley Cockburn (6)
Leslie Primary School, Glenrothes

My Five Senses

I love to hear the lovely seagulls.
I love to see my tasty pizza cooking in the oven.
I love to smell my awesome pizza.
I love to touch my beautiful, hard, bearded dragon.
I love to taste everything.

Connor Westie (6)
Leslie Primary School, Glenrothes

My Five Senses

I love to see Mum smiling.
I love to hear my dog bark.
I love to touch my glasses.
I love to smell sweets.
I love to taste soup.

Brandon Baird (6)
Leslie Primary School, Glenrothes

My Five Senses

I love to see the sun.
I love to hear the tractor in the field.
I love to touch my cat but not his paw.
I love to smell cake.
I love to taste banana.

Alix Casey (6)
Leslie Primary School, Glenrothes

Our School

I can see blue, smooth chairs,
I can hear Mrs Ewen Benn's laugh,
I can smell Mrs Nicholson's lovely wedges,
I can touch my interesting book.

Jaime-Leigh Tyler/Duffield (6)
Manor Fields Primary School, Salisbury

Our School

I can see really hard doors,
I can hear loud cars,
I can smell cold air,
I can touch wavy trees.

I can see a metal sign,
I can hear soft wind,
I can smell delicious dinners,
I can touch soft tables.

Elisa Rogers
Manor Fields Primary School, Salisbury

Our School

I can see a big green field,
I can hear loud, slow music,
I can smell yellow potato wedges,
I can touch a green field.

I can see a soft chair,
I can hear spluttering cars,
I can smell smelly fish,
I can touch a wooden bench.

I can feel hot water,
I can hear joyful children.
I can smell a smelly bin,
I can touch cold air,
I can see a fridge,
I can smell a pink cake.

William Jonathan Pearce (6)
Manor Fields Primary School, Salisbury

Our School

I can see a beautiful painting that's on the wall,
I can hear the howling wind,
I can smell some yummy fish cooking in the kitchen,
I can touch a bumpy art work on the wall.

I can see flapping birds in the sky,
I can hear loud music which is coming from the class,
I can smell hard carrots in the basket,
I can touch hard bricks that make our school.

Holly Bray
Manor Fields Primary School, Salisbury

Untitled

I can see coloured feet that are on the wall,
I can hear the noisy buzzing of the lanterns,
I can smell rubber tyres in the library,
I can touch the smooth boxes.

I can see paper books,
I can hear Zach talking loudly,
I can smell really nice things,
I can touch my soft lunch box.

Henry Russell (6)
Manor Fields Primary School, Salisbury

Our School

I can see the soft seats that are in the library,
I can hear people chatting in the classroom,
I can smell rubbery tyres that smell horrible,
I can touch bumpy mats that are soft.

I can see new books that are shiny,
I can hear the echoing of people's voices,
I can smell lots of extra juicy carrots that are in the snack bucket,
I can touch a rough seat that is quite hard.

Sam Richie
Manor Fields Primary School, Salisbury

My School

I can see a marshmallow bean bag
sitting in the library,
I can hear the sound of the pattering of our feet moving in the corridor,
I can smell a smelly bean bag,
I can touch a smooth tyre sitting in the library.

I can see a tall tree blowing in the breeze,
I can hear the sound of the wind,
I can feel the wind blowing through my hair,
I can smell the freshly cut grass, lovely.

Daisy Parry
Manor Fields Primary School, Salisbury

The Dark

In the dark I can see a fox.
In the dark I can hear an owl hoot.
The fox can smell a pie.
The fox can almost taste the yummy chicken pie.
The fox can almost touch the pie.
But the greedy owl flew by and grabbed the pie
into the sky.

Tiyana Muchenje (5)
Milverton House Preparatory School, Nuneaton

My Sister

When Isabella is on holiday she looks like
a brown berry,
Her skin is soft and warm
And she smells like strawberries,
She sounds so beautiful,
And she tastes like strawberries too.

Sophia Marsh (6)
Milverton House Preparatory School, Nuneaton

My Ponies

My ponies feel like teddy bears,
They smell like strawberries,
They are soft to the touch,
They look really beautiful,
They taste of delicious coconuts.

Nicole Wood (6)
Milverton House Preparatory School, Nuneaton

The Core Of The Earth

The core of the earth looks hard and rocky,
It feels like it will explode,
It smells like a rock,
It sounds hollow,
If I were to eat it, it would be like an
everlasting gobstopper!

Myles Alexander Hellwig (7)
Milverton House Preparatory School, Nuneaton

My Monster

My monster feels like a big soft marshmallow,
He smells like vanilla ice cream,
He is always soft to touch,
He tastes like strawberries,
He looks like a blue furry creature.

Milo Peacock (7)
Milverton House Preparatory School, Nuneaton

Pandas

Pandas climb trees and they taste like
vanilla ice cream,
When I touch them their fur is so soft,
They look like black and white cats,
They sound like a bamboo whistle,
Their smell reminds me of the jungle.

Lara Underhill (6)
Milverton House Preparatory School, Nuneaton

Snow White

Snow White looks beautiful,
She tastes like a nice juicy apple,
She smells like fruit too,
Snow White sounds like a bird whistling in the breeze,
Snow White feels like soft snow.

Grace Knight (7)
Milverton House Preparatory School, Nuneaton

Minecraft

Minecraft looks like men,
It feels like a huge world,
It tastes fun!
It smells exciting,
You can hear me cheer when I play.

Georgie Samuel Richardson (7)
Milverton House Preparatory School, Nuneaton

Rainbows

Rainbows look like colourful sweets,
Rainbows are stretchy and soft to touch,
They smell like fresh sugar,
And sound like rain pattering,
They taste just like sweet sugar.

Erin Elliott (7)
Milverton House Preparatory School, Nuneaton

The Dark

I can hear an owl hooting.
I can smell perfume.
I can hear a fox.
Dark is wonderful.
Dark looks like black stars
Dark tastes like mint.
I feel warm in my blanket.
I can smell wool.

Shaan Rai (6)
Milverton House Preparatory School, Nuneaton

The Dark

I can hear silence and peace.
It tastes like chocolate.
I can hear twit-twoo
The dark looks black and it feels like
a snuggly blanket.
The moon looks like a white button.

Ria Sanghera (6)
Milverton House Preparatory School, Nuneaton

The Dark

The dark tastes like sausages
The dark feels like cold
The dark smells like fire
The dark sounds like twit-twoo
The dark looks like a black blanket.

Oskar Metcalfe (6)
Milverton House Preparatory School, Nuneaton

The Dark

As the sun goes to sleep, the dark sets in and
night-time falls.
It becomes dark, as cool night-time air can be, smelling fresh and crisp like
a cucumber.
Bright, shiny stars twinkle like a diamond
up above the sky.
In the midst of the dark, dogs bark and the owls can be heard hooting *twit-twoo.*

Nomonde Matida Musoko (6)
Milverton House Preparatory School, Nuneaton

The Dark

Dark looks like fireworks bursting up in the sky.
Dark smells like yucky breath.
Dark feels like slime.
Dark tastes like cake.
In the dark I hear owls, bats, wind and footsteps.

Nishita Srinivas (5)
Milverton House Preparatory School, Nuneaton

Dark Is Fun

Dark is fun because I can see stars.
Dark is scary because you can see real bats.
I love the dark we can play hide-and-seek.
I can hear fireworks and silence.
I can touch space, the air tastes icy, it's cold
and smells frosty.

Mya Jade Kirkbride (6)
Milverton House Preparatory School, Nuneaton

The Dark

The dark sounds like twit-twooing owls
and beeping crickets.
The dark feels cold and scary.
The dark looks like black clouds.
The dark smells like black smoke.
The dark tastes plain, like nothing at all.

Ibrahim Ahmad (6)
Milverton House Preparatory School, Nuneaton

Bedtime

The dark makes me scared.
It's pitch-black as I lay there staring and thinking...
and worrying
Wow! Did you hear that? Was someone there?
I shiver, is it a massive monster?
Something is under my bed and moving out!
It's jumped up! Phew,
It's just Guinness the cat.

Alyx Bakewell-Beards (6)
Milverton House Preparatory School, Nuneaton

The Countryside

The countryside smells like petrol,
The countryside looks like an enormous farm,
It sounds like cars racing past,
It tastes like my dad's feet!
All over it is slushy to touch.

Megan Cook (7)
Milverton House Preparatory School, Nuneaton

Rainbows

Rainbows feel like soft velvet,
Rainbows taste like fruit,
Rainbows sound like a bird whistling in the breeze,
Rainbows smell like fresh colours,
Rainbows look like colourful patterns.

Mya Khela (7)
Milverton House Preparatory School, Nuneaton

Football

Football smells like fresh air,
Football feels very hard,
Football sounds like people cheering,
Football looks like a huge trophy!
Football tastes like water.

Ewan Robert Pearce (7)
Milverton House Preparatory School, Nuneaton

Five Senses Walk

As I walk through the zoo,
First I see an elephant,
Next I hear stomping,
Then I smell smelly smells,
Finally I touch ice cream.

Georgie Leigh Goldswain (5)
Summerhill Infant School, Bristol

Untitled

I can hear trees rustling in the wind,
Long green grass, swaying in the wind,
I touch the pavement, it's hard and rough,
I eat a snack on the way, a banana that is soft,
I smell the lovely smell of the flowers, they smell lovely.

Catherine Perkins (6)
Summerhill Infant School, Bristol

Untitled

As I walk through the zoo,
I can smell animals,
I can see animals,
I can taste the animals' food,
I can feel the animals' hard skin,
I can hear elephants, stomping more and more.

Kian Thomas Maggs (6)
Summerhill Infant School, Bristol

The Park

As I walk through the park I see
Children playing on the slides.
The children sound loud and they
come and play with us.
I can see children feeding the ducks.
I can see parents watching their children
feeding the ducks.
I can smell children.
I can hear quacking ducks.
I can smell ice cream.

Naila Rouf
Summerhill Infant School, Bristol

A Walk Through The Park

I can touch a beautiful red rose, lying on
the green grass.
I can hear wind, it's very windy and stormy,
I can see the shiny, bright sun in the sky,
I can taste sticky, squelchy, sweet strawberry jam,
I can smell sticky, squelchy mud.

Ella Heaton (6)
Summerhill Infant School, Bristol

Cats

My cat smells like hay bales,
That remind me of sunny days,
He looks like a badger,
With his black and white face,
My cat tastes like sweet honey,
And soft marshmallows,
My cat feels as soft as a blanket,
My cat looks like a tough nut chasing after his tail.

Paulina Wojciechowska (5)
Tremoilet VCP, Carmarthen

Chocolate

Chocolate smells like milk.
Chocolate sounds like a stick snapping.
Chocolate looks like brown sweets.
Chocolate tastes like milk.

Sion Bevan
Tremoilet VCP, Carmarthen

Spring

Spring looks like grass,
growing in the garden.
Spring sounds like rain,
on my window.
Spring smells like flowers,
blowing in the wind.
Spring tastes like fresh water,
from the tap.
Spring feels like a warm quilt,
on my bed.

Corey William Mayes (7)
Tremoilet VCP, Carmarthen

Spring

Spring looks like rain on the window.
Spring sounds like the wind in the trees.
Spring smells like flowers growing in
the school garden.
Spring tastes like chocolate cake.
Spring feels like the breeze howling outside in
the garden.

Paige Capp
Tremoilet VCP, Carmarthen

Spring

Spring smells like snowdrops.
Spring looks like soft mud and animals in brown fields.
Spring sounds like rain on the window.
Spring tastes like Easter eggs and yummy pancakes.
Spring feels like soft grass under my feet.

Tomos Davies
Tremoilet VCP, Carmarthen

My Dog

My dog smells like wet mud,
But after a bath he smells of roses.
My dog looks like a pumpkin,
Small, round, orange and white.
My dog sounds like a growling fox,
And a ball bumping down the stairs.
My dog tastes like an orange,
Lovely, nice and sweet.
My dog feels like soft, shiny silk,
All soft and smooth.

William Sankey
Tremoilet VCP, Carmarthen

Young Writers Information

We hope you have enjoyed reading this book – and that you will continue to in the coming years.

If you're a young writer who enjoys reading and creative writing, or the parent of an enthusiastic poet or story writer, do visit our website **www.youngwriters.co.uk**. Here you will find free competitions, workshops and games, as well as recommended reads, a poetry glossary and our blog.

If you would like to order further copies of this book, or any of our other titles give us a call or visit **www.youngwriters.co.uk**.

Young Writers
Remus House
Coltsfoot Drive
Peterborough
PE2 9BF

(01733) 890066
info@youngwriters.co.uk

Share your feelings verse any time!